Y0-AEX-432

CARAMEL PUDDING

Kathryn M. Geissinger, Ephrata, PA

2 Tbsp. butter or *margarine*
½ cup brown sugar
1 cup milk
1 Tbsp. cornstarch
1 egg, beaten
1 Tbsp. cold water
1 tsp. vanilla
Pinch salt
2 bananas, sliced
½ cup chopped nuts

1. Cook butter and sugar together over medium heat until smooth and bubbly.
2. In a medium bowl combine milk, cornstarch and egg, beating until smooth.
3. Carefully add cold water to butter and sugar mixture. Gradually add milk mixture, stirring constantly over medium heat until mixture thickens and begins to boil.
4. Remove from heat and stir in vanilla and salt. Cool slightly and pour into serving dish.
5. Top with sliced bananas and chopped nuts and serve.

Makes 2-4 servings

Brown Sugar Tapioca

Martha Bender, New Paris, IN

3 Tbsp. minute tapioca
1 cup brown sugar
⅛ tsp. salt
2 cups water
¾ tsp. vanilla
1 cup whipped topping

1. In a saucepan combine tapioca, brown sugar, salt and water. Bring to a boil and stir until tapioca appears clear. Remove from heat and stir in vanilla.
2. Cool and serve with whipped topping.

Makes 6-8 servings

My poor fingers were so sore after working on my first quilting project. I could not understand how the other women could work so quickly and have such tiny, neat stitches. My teacher finally came over and checked my quilting thread. I had been appliqueing with a spool of carpet thread!

Linda Miles, Dumfries, VA

Frozen Strawberry Dessert

Alma Miller, Partridge, KS

Crust

2 cups flour
1 cup chopped nuts
½ cup brown sugar
¾ cup margarine

Filling

1½ pints strawberries
1 cup strawberry gelatin
¾ cup sugar
8-oz. pkg. cream cheese
1 quart whipping cream

1. Combine all crust ingredients and mix well. Press into 9" x 13" baking pan.
2. Bake at 350° for 15-20 minutes. Cool.
3. To prepare filling bring ½ of strawberries to a boil in ¾-inch of water in a saucepan. Dissolve gelatin in cooked strawberries. Fold in remaining berries and cool.
4. Cream together sugar and cream cheese and mix with strawberry gelatin mixture. Chill until slightly congealed.
5. Whip cream and fold into mixture. Pour over cooled crust.
6. Freeze before serving.

Makes 12-15 servings

Rhubarb Pastry

Patti Boston, Coshocton, OH

Crust

8 Tbsp. butter, softened
1 Tbsp. sugar
1 egg yolk
1 cup flour
¼ tsp. salt
½ tsp. vanilla

Filling

2 cups fresh, diced rhubarb
2 Tbsp. butter
4 Tbsp. flour
1½ cups sugar
2 eggs, beaten
1 cup heavy cream

1. Mix together all crust ingredients and pat into 9-inch square baking pan.
2. Spread diced rhubarb over crust.
3. Combine all remaining filling ingredients and pour over rhubarb.
4. Bake at 350° for 1 hour or until set.

Makes 8-10 servings

Apple Dumplings Supreme

Ruth Meyer, Linn, KS

Pastry

2¼ cups sifted flour
¾ tsp. salt
¾ cup shortening
5 Tbsp. cold water

Apples

6 medium tart apples
½ cup sugar
1½ tsp. cinnamon
2 Tbsp. butter

Syrup

1 cup sugar
2 cups water
4 Tbsp. butter
¼ tsp. cinnamon

1. To prepare pastry sift together flour and salt. Cut in shortening. Add cold water and form into ball. Roll dough out into large rectangle and cut into 6 equal squares.
2. Peel and core apples. Place whole apple in center of each square.
3. Combine ½ cup sugar and 1½ tsp. cinnamon and fill cavity of each apple with this mixture. Dot with butter.
4. With water moisten 4 points of each pastry square and bring opposite points up over apple, overlapping them. Seal well. Arrange about 2 inches apart in 9" x 13" baking pan.
5. To prepare syrup combine all ingredients in a saucepan. Bring to a boil and boil for 3 minutes. Pour hot syrup over apples.
5. Bake at 425° for 40-45 minutes.

Makes 6 servings

I do custom quilting. Several years ago a gentleman brought me two quilt tops. After his wife died, he discovered that she had saved his neckties for 50 years. Using the neckties, he designed quilt blocks, piecing them all by hand. He chose to make the entire quilt with silk and brought me silk thread for the quilting. He had done beautiful work and gave the two quilts to his son and daughter as Christmas gifts.

Erma Landis, Sterling, IL

BROWN. SUGAR

CRANBERRY APPLE GOODIE

Lois Stoltzfus, Honey Brook, PA

Batter

½ cup sugar
1 Tbsp. flour
⅛ tsp. salt
1 tsp. cinnamon
4 cups sliced apples
⅓ cup fresh or *frozen cranberries*

Topping

1 cup uncooked oatmeal
½ cup brown sugar
½ cup flour
⅛ tsp. baking soda
⅛ tsp. baking powder
4 Tbsp. butter, melted

1. To prepare batter combine sugar, flour, salt and cinnamon. Stir into sliced apples and cranberries and spoon into baking dish.
2. To prepare topping combine all dry ingredients. Stir in butter. Spread crumb topping over apple mixture.
3. Bake at 375° for 35-40 minutes. Serve with ice cream or milk.

Makes 8 servings

Jody's Apple Walnut Crisp

Janis Landefeld, Baltimore, MD

4-5 tart apples
1 Tbsp. lemon juice
½ cup flour
½ cup brown sugar, firmly packed
¼ tsp. salt
¼ tsp. nutmeg
½ tsp. cinnamon
4 Tbsp. butter or *margarine*
½ cup chopped walnuts

1. Pare, core and thinly slice apples to measure 4 cups. Arrange in greased 8-inch square baking pan. Sprinkle with lemon juice.
2. Combine flour, sugar, salt, nutmeg and cinnamon. Work in butter until crumbly and add walnuts. Sprinkle crumb mixture evenly over apples.
3. Bake at 375° for 35-45 minutes or until topping is brown and apples are tender.
4. Serve warm with cream, whipped topping or ice cream.

Makes 6 servings

Fruit Pizza

Elizabeth J. Yoder, Millersburg, OH
Lola Kennel, Strang, NE

¾ cup sugar
8 Tbsp. margarine
1 egg, beaten
1½ cups flour
1 tsp. baking powder
¼ tsp. salt
8-oz. pkg. cream cheese, softened
¼ cup sugar
½ tsp. vanilla
1 cup whipped topping
Assortment of fruit pieces

1. Cream together ¾ cup sugar, margarine and egg. Blend in flour, baking powder and salt. Pat mixture into ungreased 14-inch pizza pan.
2. Bake at 375° for 10-12 minutes or until lightly browned. Cool.
3. Cream together cream cheese, ¼ cup sugar and vanilla. Fold in whipped topping. Spread mixture over cooled crust.
4. Arrange an assortment of fruit pieces over cream cheese mixture. Glaze with an orange sauce and serve immediately.

Makes 10-12 servings

Orange Sauce

Susan Alexander, Baltimore, MD

½ cup sugar
Dash salt
1 Tbsp. cornstarch
½ cup orange juice
2 Tbsp. lemon juice
¼ cup water

1. In a small saucepan mix sugar, salt and cornstarch. Gradually add orange juice, lemon juice and water. Cook over medium heat, stirring constantly until thickened and boiling. Boil and stir 1 minute.
2. Remove from heat. Cool and spoon over fruit pizza.

Makes 1 cup sauce

S
SUGAR

Viennese Chocolate Torte

Merlie Vidette, Duxbury, MA

Torte

5-oz. pkg. semi-sweet chocolate chips
7 medium eggs, separated
¾ cup sugar
1½ cups walnuts, ground
1 handful plain bread crumbs

Frosting

3 level Tbsp. powdered sugar
1 Tbsp. butter
3 Tbsp. boiling water
4 ozs. sweet chocolate

1. Melt chocolate chips in double boiler.
2. Beat egg yolks and sugar until thick and lemon colored. Add chocolate and mix well.
3. Beat egg whites until stiff peaks form. Mix chocolate batter into egg whites by spoonsful, alternating with ground nuts and bread crumbs. Pour into greased and floured springform pan.
4. Bake at 350° for 40-45 minutes or until no longer sticky.
5. To prepare frosting combine sugar, butter and water and stir until mixture appears clear.
6. Melt chocolate in double boiler. Add to sugar mixture and stir until smooth. Pour over cake and serve.

Note: *The longer you stir the frosting, the thicker it becomes. Cake may also be served with whipped topping.*

Makes 8-10 servings

I well remember my first quilting experience with my grandmother Florence Stauffer. I was newly married and desperately wanted my stitches to be even. I pulled the needle through on the bottom and back through on the top each time. She graciously complimented my even stitches, then showed me how to guide my needle underneath with my opposite hand to accomplish even stitches on both the top and bottom.

Jul Hoober, New Holland, PA

Velvet Cheesecake

Terry Kessler, Bayside, NY

1 lb. ricotta cheese
2 8-oz. pkgs. cream cheese
1 lb. sour cream
1½ cups sugar
4 eggs
1 Tbsp. vanilla
3 Tbsp. cornstarch
3 Tbsp. flour
8 Tbsp. butter, melted

1. Cream together ricotta cheese, cream cheese, sour cream and sugar. Add eggs, one at a time. Add vanilla and mix well.
2. While mixer is still going, sprinkle cornstarch and flour around sides of bowl. Mix in melted butter. (Batter should be thin.) Pour into greased 9-inch springform pan.
3. Bake at 325° for 1 hour. Turn off oven and let cheesecake set for 2 hours. Remove from oven and chill before taking out of pan.

Makes 10-12 servings

DANISH PASTRY PUFFS

Joyce Niemann, Fruitland Park, FL

Pastry Puffs

16 Tbsp. butter or *margarine*
2 cups flour
2 Tbsp. ice water
1 cup water
1 tsp. almond extract
3 eggs

Frosting

2 cups powdered sugar
Milk
½ cup chopped nuts

The summer I turned 14, I kept house for my recently widowed grandfather in the Finger Lakes region of New York. At the end of the summer my parents arrived from Massachusetts to take me home. For the occasion I decided to make a spice cake. I doubled the amount of raisins and nuts, assuming twice as many would be twice as good. In my rush I also tried to frost it before it was cool. The cake was much too soggy and sweet to eat. I remember that as the day I learned to follow recipes.

Sara Harter Fredette, Williamsburg, MA

1. To prepare puffs cut 8 Tbsp. butter into 1 cup flour with pastry blender until mixture resembles coarse meal. Sprinkle ice water, 1 Tbsp. at a time, evenly over surface. Stir with a fork until dry ingredients are moistened.
2. Divide dough in half. Pat each half into 3" x 12" rectangle on lightly greased baking sheet. Set pastry aside.
3. Place remaining 8 Tbsp. butter and 1 cup water in saucepan. Bring to a boil. Stir in almond extract. Reduce heat to low and add remaining 1 cup flour, stirring vigorously until mixture leaves sides of pan and forms a smooth ball. Remove from heat and cool slightly.
4. Add eggs, one at a time, and beat with spoon after each addition. Beat until batter is smooth. Spread evenly over pastry rectangles.
5. Bake at 350° for 55-60 minutes until golden.
6. To prepare frosting combine powdered sugar with milk until spreading consistency. (Do not use too much milk.) Spread pastry puffs with frosting and sprinkle with chopped nuts.

Makes 12 servings

Walnut Glory Cake

Ella G. Wenger, New Holland, PA

¾ cup flour
1 tsp. salt
2 tsp. cinnamon
9 eggs, separated
1½ cups sugar
2 tsp. vanilla
2 cups finely chopped walnuts

1. Sift flour with salt and cinnamon. Set aside.
2. In a large mixing bowl beat egg whites until soft peaks form. Gradually add ¾ cup sugar and continue beating until very stiff.
3. In separate bowl combine egg yolks, ¾ cup sugar and vanilla. Beat until thick. Stir in dry ingredients. Gently fold this batter into egg whites. Fold in walnuts and spoon into 10-inch tube pan.
4. Bake at 350° for 55-60 minutes. This cake resembles angel food cake.

Makes 16-20 servings

Surprise Chocolate Cake

Betty Richards, Rapid City, SD

Cake

16 Tbsp. margarine, softened
4 Tbsp. cocoa
2 cups sugar
4 eggs
1½ cups flour
¼ tsp. salt
1 tsp. baking powder
1½ tsp. vanilla
1½ cups pecans (optional)
1 bag miniature marshmallows

Frosting

4 Tbsp. margarine
½ cup evaporated milk
Dash salt
1-lb. box powdered sugar
½ cup cocoa
1 tsp. vanilla

1. To prepare cake combine margarine, cocoa, sugar, eggs (one at a time), flour, salt, baking powder, vanilla and pecans in mixing bowl. Spread mixture into greased 9" x 13" baking pan.
2. Bake at 350° for 30-40 minutes. Remove from oven and immediately pour marshmallows evenly over top.
3. To prepare frosting combine margarine, milk and salt in a saucepan and bring to a boil. Boil slowly for 1 minute.
4. Sift powdered sugar and stir in cocoa. Add to hot milk mixture. Add vanilla and beat until smooth. (If frosting seems too thick, add more milk.) While still hot, pour evenly over marshmallows. Cool and serve.

Makes 20-24 servings

I was a homemaker with time on my hands when I began piecing quilts. My mother had taught me to sew so I began with a simple Log Cabin quilt. A friend from Massachusetts sent me a photograph of a Sampler and asked whether I would be willing to piece one for her. After checking numerous quilt books for the many different patterns, I finally completed it. I felt as though I should have about a thousand dollars for it! At the time that would have been an unheard of price. However, I'm glad I took on the challenge, as piecing Samplers has become my personal quilt specialty.

Naomi Lapp, New Holland, PA

FLOUR
APPLE
SAUC
NUTMEG

Applesauce Cake

Jeanette E. Barthold, Bethlehem, PA

1¾ cups coarsely chopped walnuts
1¾ cups raisins
3½ cups sifted flour
2 tsp. baking soda
¼ tsp. salt
1½ tsp. cinnamon
1 tsp. ground cloves
1 tsp. ginger
¼ tsp. nutmeg
1 cup butter
2 cups sugar
2 large eggs
2 cups applesauce

1. Dredge nuts and raisins in ¼ cup flour. Set aside.
2. Sift together remaining flour, baking soda, salt and spices. Set aside.
3. Cream butter until light and fluffy. Gradually add sugar. Beat in eggs, one at a time. Add dry ingredients, alternating with applesauce and beginning and ending with dry ingredients. Fold in nuts and raisins. Spoon batter into well-greased and floured 9-inch tube pan.
4. Bake at 350° for 1 hour and 25 minutes, or until cake feels springy and has pulled away from sides. Invert and cool.
5. Cut into small slices and serve.

Makes 16-20 servings

Chocolate Mint Cake

Janet Groff, Stevens, PA

Cake

2 cups flour
2 cups sugar
1 tsp. baking powder
2 tsp. baking soda
¼ tsp. salt
½ cup cocoa
½ cup cooking oil
1 cup strong liquid coffee
1 cup milk
1 tsp. vanilla
2 eggs

Mint Frosting

2 cups powdered sugar
½ cup soft butter or *margarine*
3 Tbsp. creme de menthe syrup

Glaze

6-oz. pkg. chocolate chips
6 Tbsp. butter or *margarine*

1. To prepare cake batter sift all dry ingredients together. Add remaining ingredients and beat 2 minutes. Pour into a 9" x 13" baking pan.
2. Bake at 350° for 40-45 minutes or until wooden pick inserted in center comes out clean. Cool on wire rack.
3. To prepare mint frosting beat all ingredients until light and fluffy. Spread frosting on cooled cake.
4. To prepare glaze melt chocolate chips and butter together. Cool slightly and spread over mint frosting layer.
5. Chill in refrigerator 10-15 minutes. Remove and store at room temperature.

Variation: *Substitute 1 cup buttermilk for the milk and omit the mint frosting layer.*

Lucille Brubacker, Barnett, MO

Makes 20-24 servings

When our daughter was expecting a baby, I put together a Little Lamb baby quilt. She surprised everyone, including her doctor, and gave birth to twin daughters. Needless to say, I quickly went to work on the second Little Lamb baby quilt.

Elsie Long, Sterling, IL

Cranberry Shortcake

Betsy Jevon, Pittsburgh, PA

Shortcake

1 cup flour
¾ cup sugar
1 tsp. baking powder
2 Tbsp. shortening
1½ cups fresh cranberries
½ cup milk

Hot Butter Sauce

½ cup butter or *margarine*
½ cup brown sugar
½ cup heavy cream
½ tsp. vanilla

1. To prepare shortcake sift together flour, sugar and baking powder. Cut in shortening. Carefully fold in cranberrries. Add milk and mix lightly. Spoon into greased 8-inch square baking pan.
2. Bake at 375° for 30 minutes.
3. To prepare butter sauce melt butter. Stir in brown sugar until it dissolves. Add cream and vanilla and heat slowly. Do not bring to a boil.
4. Serve hot shortcake with hot butter sauce.

Makes 8 servings

MILK
BUTTER
FRESH
CRANBERRIES

Poppy Seed Cake

Rosaria V. Strachan, Old Greenwich, CT

Cake

16 Tbsp. butter
8-oz. pkg. cream cheese
1½ cups sugar
1½ tsp. vanilla
4 eggs
2½ cups flour
1½ tsp. baking powder
½ cup raisins
1 cup finely chopped walnuts

Filling

¼ cup poppy seeds
¼ cup sugar
1 tsp. lemon rind
¼ tsp. vanilla

1. In large bowl cream together butter and cream cheese until light and fluffy. Add sugar and vanilla and beat 5 minutes. Add eggs, one at a time, beating after each addition.
2. Sift together flour and baking powder. Add to creamed mixture. Fold in raisins and walnuts. Spoon ½ of batter into greased 10-cup bundt pan.
3. To prepare filling combine all ingredients. Sprinkle filling over batter in bundt pan and top with remaining batter. Using a knife, swirl to spread filling throughout.
4. Bake at 325° for 65-70 minutes.

Makes 16-20 servings

Lemon Sauce for Pound Cake

Melinda Moritz, Flourtown, PA

4 eggs, beaten
2 cups sugar
8 Tbsp. butter
1 Tbsp. grated lemon rind
½ cup lemon juice

1. Combine all ingredients in saucepan. Cook over medium heat, stirring constantly until mixture is thick and bubbly, about 10 minutes.
2. Chill and serve with pound cake.

Makes 3 cups sauce

Rich Pound Cake

Joan T. Schneider, Seaford, NY

16 Tbsp. margarine
2 cups sugar
4 eggs, separated
3 cups flour
3 tsp. baking powder
½ tsp. salt
1 cup milk

1. Cream together margarine, sugar and egg yolks.
2. Sift together flour, baking powder and salt. Add flour mixture to creamed mixture, alternating with milk.
3. Beat egg whites until stiff. Carefully fold into batter. Put into greased 10-inch bundt pan.
4. Bake at 350° for 1 hour.

Makes 16-20 servings

Pumpkin Whoopie Pies

Lydia Brubacker, Barnett, MO

Cookie Dough

2 cups brown sugar
1 cup cooking oil
1½ cups cooked and mashed pumpkin
2 eggs
3 cups flour
1 tsp. salt
1 tsp. baking powder
1 tsp. baking soda
1 tsp. vanilla
1½ Tbsp. cinnamon
½ Tbsp. ginger
½ Tbsp. ground cloves

Filling

3 cups shortening
4 cups powdered sugar
1 Tbsp. milk
4 egg whites, beaten
4 Tbsp. flour
2 Tbsp. vanilla

1. Cream together brown sugar and oil. Add pumpkin and eggs and mix well.
2. Combine all remaining ingredients and mix into creamed mixture. Drop by large tablespoonsful onto greased baking sheet.
3. Bake at 350° for 10-12 minutes.
4. To prepare filling combine all ingredients and mix well.
5. Make whoopie pies by spreading filling on flat side of one cookie and making a sandwich with another cookie. Store in airtight container.

Makes 2 dozen cookies

I belong to St. James Lutheran Church in Pleasantville, Pennsylvania. About five years ago our pastor was a young, single woman. She decided to get married and planned to move to Harrisburg. Even though only two of us had ever made a quilt, the congregation decided to make a quilt as a combination going-away and wedding gift. We planned to surprise her, but because she was constantly visiting people, it became increasingly difficult. We told her about the quilt and she joined in the fun. We had several potluck suppers and lunches with lots of laughter and joy as we worked together on what became for all of us a labor of love.

Theresa Leppert, Schellsburg, PA

Mellowy Moments Tea Cookies

Ann Bateman, Arnprior, ON
Doreen Copeland, Florence, SC

1 cup butter
1½ cups brown sugar
1 egg
1 tsp. vanilla
2 cups flour
1 tsp. baking soda
Pinch salt

1. Cream together butter and brown sugar. Add egg and vanilla and mix well.
2. Sift together flour, baking soda and salt. Add to creamed mixture and mix well.
3. Drop by teaspoonsful onto greased baking sheet. Flatten slightly with fork.
4. Bake at 350° for 8-10 minutes or until cookies are light brown.

Makes 5 dozen cookies

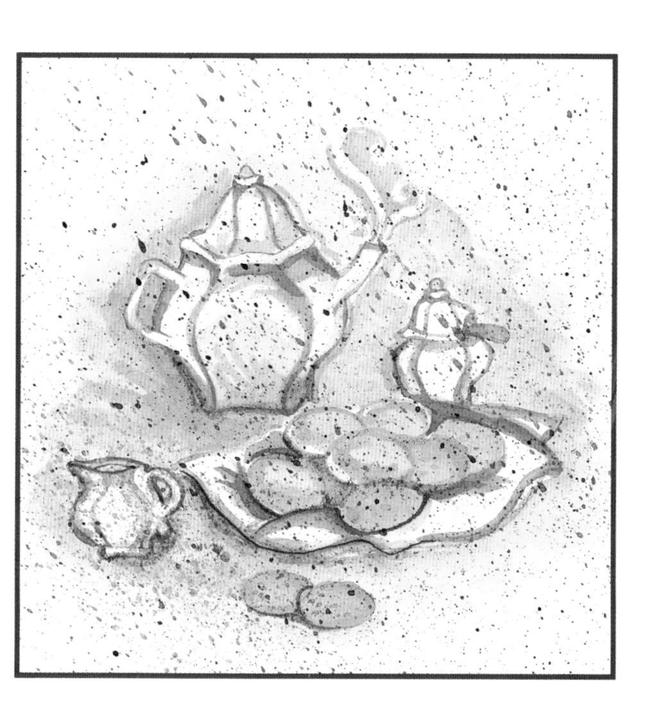

Grandma's Molasses Cookies

Verda Wilsman, Pittsburgh, PA

1 cup shortening
1 cup white sugar
1 cup molasses
5 cups flour
1 Tbsp. ginger
1 Tbsp. cinnamon
1 tsp. salt
1 Tbsp. baking soda
½ cup warm water

1. Cream together shortening, sugar and molasses. Add flour and spices and mix well.
2. Dissolve baking soda in water and add to batter, mixing well.
3. Roll out to ½-inch thickness onto floured waxed paper. Using 2¼-inch cookie cutter, cut out cookies. Arrange on greased cookie sheet.
4. Bake at 350° for 15 minutes.
5. Transfer from cookie sheet to tin container while cookies are still warm, arranging in layers between waxed paper. (This will keep cookies soft.)

Makes 6 dozen cookies

Lebkuchen

Merlie Vidette, Duxbury, MA

Cookie Dough

2¾ cups flour
1 cup.brown sugar
¼ tsp. baking soda
5 Tbsp. honey
½ tsp. cinnamon
½ tsp. ground cloves
½ tsp. allspice
2 eggs
Grated rind of ½ lemon

Frosting

1 egg white
Powdered sugar

1. Combine all cookie dough ingredients by hand in large bowl. Dough will be moist and slightly sticky.
2. Roll out dough, a little at a time, to ⅛-inch thickness. Cut into shapes with cookie cutter. Arrange on greased baking sheets.
3. Bake at 350° for approximately 8-10 minutes. Let cool.
4. To prepare frosting beat egg white with enough powdered sugar to make of spreading consistency.
5. Spread cooled cookies with frosting and let dry. Store in airtight container.

Note: *These cookies soften with age and increase in flavor. They have no fat and will not turn rancid.*

Makes 5-6 dozen cookies

RAISINS
BUTTER

Pinwheels

Janice Way, Warrington, PA

2 cups sifted flour
4 tsp. baking powder
½ tsp. salt
½ tsp. cream of tartar
2 tsp. sugar
½ cup shortening
⅔ cup milk
2-3 Tbsp. butter or *margarine, melted*
2 Tbsp. sugar
1 tsp. cinnamon
Raisins (optional)

1. Sift together flour, baking powder, salt, cream of tartar and 2 tsp. sugar. Cut in shortening until mixture resembles coarse crumbs. Add milk and stir until dough follows fork around bowl.
2. Turn out onto lightly floured surface. Knead gently for ½ minute. Roll out dough to ¼-inch thickness.
3. Spread with melted butter. Sprinkle with 2 Tbsp. sugar, cinnamon and raisins. Roll up and seal edges. Cut into ½-inch slices. Arrange, cut side down, on greased baking sheet.
4. Bake at 450° for 12-15 minutes.

Makes 4 dozen cookies

Sour Cream Raisin Bars

Susie Braun, Rapid City, SD
Adella Halsey, Wymore, NE
Marian Brubacker, Barnett, MO

Crust

1 cup brown sugar
1 cup butter
1 tsp. baking soda
1¾ cups uncooked oatmeal
1¾ cups flour

Filling

2 cups raisins
Water to cover
3 egg yolks, beaten
1½ cups sour cream
1 cup sugar
2 Tbsp. cornstarch

1. To prepare crust cream together brown sugar and butter. Add baking soda, oats and flour and mix well. Press ½ of mixture into 9" x 13" baking pan.
2. Bake at 350° for 7 minutes.
3. To prepare filling simmer raisins in water to cover until raisins are softened. Drain and cool.
4. In a heavy saucepan combine egg yolks, sour cream, sugar and cornstarch and cook over medium-high heat until mixture begins to thicken, stirring constantly. Remove from heat and stir in raisins. Pour over baked crust. Sprinkle remaining ½ of crust mixture over top.
5. Bake at 350° for 15-20 minutes. Cool and refrigerate until ready to serve.

Makes 20-24 bars

The quilt frame in our family is an heirloom. It was built by my great-grandfather about 1910 and used "hard" by my great-grandmother. She passed the frame to her daughter—my grandmother—who learned to enjoy quilting only after she had the frame. My mother borrowed the frame for six months and returned it to Grandmother who used it until her eyesight gave out. I inherited this family treasure, and today I almost always have a quilt in the frame.

Jennifer L. Rhodes, Lancaster, PA

Lemon Bon Bons

Alice Walker, Winter Haven, FL

Cookie Dough

6 Tbsp. butter or *margarine*
1/3 cup powdered sugar
1/4 cup cornstarch
1 1/4 cups sifted flour

Frosting

1 cup powdered sugar
1 tsp. butter
2 Tbsp. lemon juice
1 drop yellow food coloring
1/2 cup finely chopped pecans

1. To prepare dough cream together butter and powdered sugar until fluffy.
2. Sift together cornstarch and flour and add to batter, beating until well mixed. Refrigerate at least 1 hour.
3. Shape batter into walnut-sized balls. Arrange on lightly greased cookie sheet.
4. Bake at 350° for 15 minutes or until light brown. Cool before frosting.
5. To prepare frosting combine all ingredients except pecans and mix well. Spread frosting over cookies. Dip top of each cookie in finely chopped pecans.

FLOUR
10X
SUGAR

Marble Brownies

Geraldine A. Ebersole, Hershey, PA

Brownies

1 cup shortening, softened
2 cups sugar
4 eggs
1½ cups sifted flour
1 tsp. baking powder
1 tsp. salt or *less*
1 tsp. vanilla
2 ozs. unsweetened chocolate, melted

Frosting

1 oz. unsweetened chocolate
2 Tbsp. margarine
4 Tbsp. milk
2 cups sifted, powdered sugar
½ cup chopped nuts

1. Cream together shortening, sugar and eggs and blend thoroughly.
2. Sift together flour, baking powder and salt and stir into creamed mixture. Divide batter into 2 bowls.
3. To ½ of batter add vanilla and mix well.
4. To ½ of batter add melted chocolate and mix well. Spoon 2 batters into greased 9" x 13" baking pan in checkerboard fashion. Swirl slightly with spatula.
5. Bake at 350° for 35 minutes. Cool.
6. To prepare frosting melt together chocolate and margarine. Add milk and powdered sugar and beat well. Spread over brownies and sprinkle with nuts. Cut and serve.

Makes 20-24 servings

About a year ago my five-year-old twin grandsons wandered into my studio to examine the Baltimore Album squares I had hanging on my felt wall. One smartly commented, "That looks like a nice quilt you're making there, Gram." The other studied the wall a long time and said, "Gram, it needs more hearts!" So for him I have added several more squares with hearts in them.

Susan Orleman, Pittsburgh, PA

CHIPS

Deep-Dish Brownies

Mary Lou Kirtland, Berkeley Heights, NJ

¾ cup butter
1½ cups sugar
1½ cups vanilla
3 eggs
½ cup flour
½ cup cocoa
½ tsp. baking powder
½ tsp. salt
1 cup peanut butter chips

1. Cream together butter, sugar and vanilla. Add eggs and mix well. Add all dry ingredients and beat thoroughly. Fold in peanut butter chips. Spoon into lightly greased 9" x 13" baking pan.
2. Bake at 350° for 40-45 minutes until brownies begin to pull away from pan. Cool before cutting. Do not overbake.

Makes 36 small brownies

Peppermint Brownies

Marilyn Wallace, Alfred, ME
Sherry Bradley, Albuquerque, NM

Brownies

2 squares unsweetened chocolate
½ cup margarine
2 eggs
1 cup sugar
½ cup chopped nuts
½ cup flour
1 tsp. vanilla

Frosting

4 Tbsp. soft margarine
2 cups powdered sugar
½ tsp. milk
2 Tbsp. sour cream
½ tsp. peppermint extract
Drop green food coloring

Glaze

2 squares unsweetened chocolate
2 Tbsp. margarine

1. To prepare brownies melt chocolate and margarine together.
2. Combine all other ingredients and add to chocolate mixture. Mix thoroughly. Pour into 8-inch square baking pan.
3. Bake at 350° for 20-25 minutes. Cool.
4. To prepare frosting combine all ingredients and mix well. Spread over cooled brownies and let stand until frosting sets.
5. To prepare glaze melt chocolate and margarine together. Drizzle over frosting and tilt pan to spread thinly. Cut into bars and serve.

Makes 24 small brownies

About twenty years ago my grandmother pieced a scrap quilt using fabric from the clothes I had worn as a child. My mother told me about two sisters in rural Jackson County, Tennessee who did quilting for people. When they had quilted my top, I drove out to their home to pick it up. I had not previously negotiated a price (which was foolish). They began apologizing, saying they would have to charge me extra for the binding. They asked for $6.00. I gasped and offered to pay them more, as I felt it was worth at least $75.00. Refusing to take the extra money, they explained to me that quilting was something they loved, not something they did to make money. Today these two industrious women are in their 90s and still quilting because they love it.

Jane L. Murphy, Malvern, PA

INDEX

The Best of

FAVORITE RECIPES FROM QUILTERS

DESSERTS

CAKES, COOKIES, PUDDINGS

Louise Stoltzfus

Good Books
Intercourse, PA 17534
Printed and bound in Hong Kong

Cover design and illustrations by Cheryl Benner
Design by Dawn J. Ranck

DESSERTS: THE BEST OF FAVORITE RECIPES FROM QUILTERS

International Standard Book Number: 1-56148-116-5
Library of Congress Catalog Card Number: 94-14898

Library of Congress Cataloging-in-Publication Data

Desserts : cakes, cookies, puddings / [compiled by] Louise Stoltzfus.
p. cm. — (The Best of Favorite recipes from quilters)
Includes index.
ISBN 1-56148-116-5 : $7.95
1. Desserts. I. Stoltzfus, Louise, 1952- . II. Series.
TX773.D4779 1994
641.8'6–dc20 94-14898
CIP

Introduction

Amid the rush and haste of life, many people seek rest and quiet in community life. Quilters find community in common goals and activities. They talk of needles and thread, fabric and stitches, and bedcovers and pieces of art. They gather in homes, fabric shops, and convention centers to share their ideas and projects.

Many quilters are also homemakers. Some treat both cooking and quilting as high art forms. Others work hard to prepare varied and healthful meals for their busy families and quilt when they have free time.

From Chocolate Pudding Dessert to Cranberry Shortcake to Lemon Bon Bons, these Dessert recipes are both practical and delicious. Those who love to quilt and those who love to cook will share in the special vibrancy of this small collection.

Punch Bowl Trifle

Joan Coale Klosek, Ellicott City, MD
Fanny E. Hymes, Clarksville, MD

1 pound cake
1 small pkg. instant vanilla pudding
21-oz. can cherry pie filling
20-oz. can pineapple sauce or *crushed pineapple*
12-oz. carton whipped topping
1 small jar maraschino cherries, drained
Crushed walnuts (optional)

1. Cut cake in half. Cut ½ of cake into small cubes and line bottom of glass punch bowl.
2. Prepare pudding according to directions. Pour ½ of pudding over cake cubes. Pour ½ of pie filling over pudding. Pour ½ of pineapple over pie filling. Top with ½ of whipped topping. Repeat layers, beginning with remaining ½ of cake.
3. Garnish with maraschino cherries and sprinkle with nuts if desired. Refrigerate at least 4 hours to set. Serve.

Makes 12-16 servings

Rice Pudding with Lemon Sauce

Mary Pat Sloan, Downingtown, PA

Pudding

3 cups milk
1½ Tbsp. butter or *margarine*
⅓ cup white sugar
3 eggs
2 cups uncooked rice
⅛ tsp. salt
½ tsp. vanilla
⅛ tsp. nutmeg
¼ cup raisins

Lemon Sauce

½ cup white sugar
2 Tbsp. cornstarch
1 cup water
4 Tbsp. butter
3 Tbsp. lemon juice
1 tsp. grated lemon rind

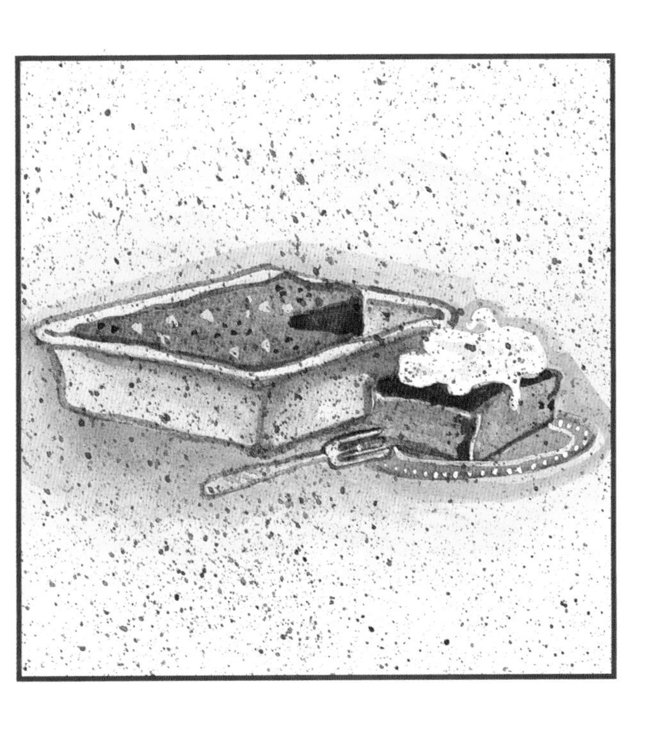

HONEYCOMB PUDDING

Judy Sharer, Port Matilda, PA

8 Tbsp. butter or *margarine, softened*
½ cup sugar
½ cup sour milk
½ cup flour
½ cup molasses
4 eggs, well beaten
1 tsp. baking soda
¼ cup hot water
1 cup whipped topping

1. Mix together butter, sugar, sour milk, flour and molasses. Stir in eggs.
2. Dissolve baking soda in hot water. Add to pudding mixture and stir until blended. Pour into 1½-quart baking dish.
3. Bake at 350° for 30 minutes or until center springs back when touched.
4. Cool and serve with whipped topping.

Makes 6-8 servings

Graham Cracker Pudding

Ruth Ann Hoover, New Holland, PA

2 egg yolks
½ cup sugar
⅔ cup milk
1 pkg. unflavored gelatin
½ cup cold water
2 egg whites, beaten
2 cups whipped topping
1 tsp. vanilla
14 graham crackers, crushed
3 Tbsp. butter, melted

1. In a saucepan beat egg yolks. Add sugar and milk and cook until slightly thickened.
2. Dissolve gelatin in cold water. Pour hot mixture over gelatin and stir until smooth. Chill for 20-30 minutes.
3. Beat egg whites until soft peaks form. Fold into chilled gelatin mixture. Fold whipped topping into mixture. Add vanilla.
4. Combine crushed graham crackers with melted butter. Reserve ½ cup crumbs.
5. Arrange graham cracker crumbs across bottom of 8-inch square baking dish. Pour pudding mixture over crackers. Top with reserved crumbs and serve.

Makes 6-8 servings

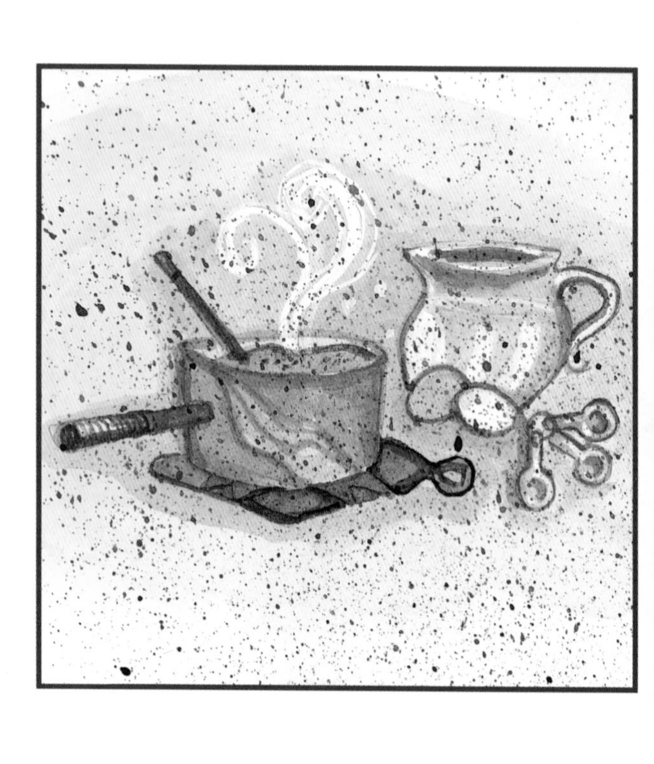

1. To prepare pudding scald milk. Add butter and sugar. Set aside to cool.
2. Lightly beat eggs. Slowly pour milk mixture into eggs. Stir in rice, salt, vanilla, nutmeg and raisins.
3. Pour into greased baking dish. Set into pan of hot water.
4. Bake at 325° for 45-60 minutes.
5. To prepare lemon sauce combine sugar and cornstarch in a saucepan. Add water and heat mixture, stirring constantly until it comes to a boil. Reduce heat and simmer for 3 minutes.
6. Remove from heat; stir in butter, lemon juice and rind. Chill. Pour over rice pudding and serve.

Makes 10 servings

My friend and I each have sons on our local school soccer team. One day they stood talking on the field. Kyle reached over and started pulling threads off my son Brian's clothing. He asked, "Does your mother quilt?" My son came home quite displeased with his decorated clothes. Kyle, not knowing that we knew each other, hurried home to his mother with the news that he had found a new quilting friend for her.

Marilyn Mowry, Irving, TX

Chocolate Pudding Dessert

Esther Lapp, Sterling, IL

1 cup sugar or *less*
2 Tbsp. cocoa
2 tsp. flour
¾ cup hot water
1 tsp. vanilla
Pinch salt
1 cup flour
2 Tbsp. cocoa
¾ cup sugar or *less*
2 tsp. baking powder
2 Tbsp. cooking oil or *melted margarine*
⅔ cup milk
¼ cup chopped nuts or *chopped dates*

1. In a saucepan combine 1 cup sugar, 2 Tbsp. cocoa, 2 tsp. flour and hot water. Bring to a boil and cook for 1 minute. Add vanilla and salt and cool slightly.
2. In a bowl combine 1 cup flour, 2 Tbsp. cocoa, ¾ cup sugar, baking powder, oil and milk. Pour into greased 9-inch square baking pan. Sprinkle with nuts or dates. Pour hot syrup over batter.
3. Bake at 350° for 25-30 minutes or until baked through.
4. Serve with ice cream or whipped topping.

Makes 6-8 servings